couplets for a shrinking world

Sandy—

Keep spreading the couplet love!

couplets

for a

shrinking

world

John

11-5-2022

john medeiros

NORTH STAR PRESS OF ST. CLOUD, INC.
Saint Cloud, Minnesota

ISBN 978-0-87839-600-9

First Edition, June 2012

Printed in the United States of America

Published by
North Star Press of St. Cloud, Inc.
P.O. Box 451
St. Cloud, Minnesota 56302

www.northstarpress.com

for my twin brother, Bobby,
and the rest of my family . . .

table of contents

one

two

couplets for a shrinking world

one

Facing North

I feel God only
as the stones feel the hard crush.

Cain, Ed Ingebretsen

I have looked for heroes in the seaweed.
Searched for tongues in the ocean's waves

blue & green & wet with nature's fury.
All to find him.

I swear he was there once, lobster-trapped
along the shores of Narragansett Bay,

where I ran for three miles at 5 A.M. The weight
of the wind heart-heavy against my chest.

Tired victims seek refuge
by facing north.

& I took him in like a secret breath—
& surrounded myself with holy water.

Faced the monastery to the north
(as if the north would protect me from myself).

Then, like parted waters, my body split in two—
One half crushed by his weight,

the other, long detached like an unknown twin
before dawn has planned her dirty day.

Mercy

An open hand, the sky never succumbing to its gravity. The bee swarms around the hive
like an apology waiting to happen.

& if he listens closely he can hear the faint *click click clack* of the streetlight as it struggles to
define itself, reminding him it's safe to return home.

Safety never sounded so quiet.

Perhaps muscle-spasmed.
Perhaps forgiven, belt-buckled, signed & dated to validate his existence.
Perhaps never needing compassion at all.

He wants to lie down with lizards. He wants to perform that magic trick—where the
man cuts himself in half & pretends to be whole. *Hocus, pocus*, and back again.

Instead he remembers the parking lot at the end of the block, lit with cameras
& waits for the leaves of the elm tree out back to fall,
one by one like pages of a book censored.

bruise

floats to the surface like some sort of circus act
                              the freak behind the glass

whose heart, when beaten, can cause

his skin to bubble. flesh quivers,
                              veins collapse & such & such. & he

lies vasculitic in his blue-black skin,

cherry-popped, eyes bulged
                              out behind broken skin,

passers-by pretending not to notice.

Washington Suite/Inauguration

i.

Marble, concrete, coldness a sort of politic
that greets me, with half the people of the city
buried below ground half the time.

Walking graveyard,
a voice within me whispers,
all dead soldiers on their way home.

Their way home a subway color.
Their way home a subculture,
past meth houses & the National Cathedral

where no thing greens anymore.
My country 'tis of thee,
sweet land of liberty.

Outside the subway window
Potomac rips the city, now a half-
frayed edge, cheap linen, still

people pour themselves
like sand on top of sand, each
struggling for a chance just to see

the newest rock, to be first
to feel the heartbeat that pumps.
this city scatters them about, red blood

cells in a vein too long anemic.
I visit this city—
both the dead to feed my body

& the living to feed my soul.
I visit this city as it hovers
over the center of the world

shoots itself up like a drug
into hungry veins. We are its high.
It feels nothing without us.

My country,
sweet land of liberty,
of thee I sing.

ii.

Push, he says
  the wall split in half;
  like a whip, crack trickling down,
  path of tear, chronograph,
  discharge of a lover's breakdown

pouring through. & I push
  as if pushing could heal.
  I have been too selfish,
  & this is how I feel.

Push, he says
  the pillow before me a blindfold
  that lets in only red light, the color of love
  when all pain is gone, a loss foretold,
  scent of man, rubber of glove

seeping through. & still I push,
  heart open as if a beast
  to be probed, & at that moment of rush
  he stops & I release.

iii.

the blue floats to my skin
& opens like an eye
watching the world through monocle

the mark almost purple
across my bicep spreads itself
the size of a thumb

this is where he pledges
his love, the words from his lips
fall onto my arm like a heavy stone

& I, softly, *thank you*

his eyes look down as though my words
were something suddenly dropped,
& he lies wanting more

so I give, trying all the while to carry
his pain to perhaps suck it out
of him like poison from a wound

I give as if to push out from my heart
all the flowers that suddenly grow
like a thick & heavy vine.

I want only to save him.

iv.

Keys shaking in my bag as I walk remind me I've a home to return to.
      The bruise on my arm, not there just days ago, the heart that hunts
      for the right word. They tell me the visit is over.
A chauffeur holds a sign that reads Stone.

Everything matters at this moment,
      even the phone call I make to the man who enchants me, a man
      I both do & do not want to call.
Enchant, he muses, *from the Latin, meaning 'in chains.'*

This airport has similar sorrows, all of which seem vital to its existence.
      How has this terminal not collapsed with the weight of such pain?
      & everything worthwhile exists in shades of blue. Even the sunlight
      that struggles through the glass is filtered by a blue-grey screen.

An airline attendant, eyes highlighted by blue shadow,
      asks for my wallet & I show it to her, pull out the slate hide
      not knowing why it should matter, but knowing it does.
We are all equally nondescript, after all,
      no identification will fill in our blanks.

& I direct myself to a plane that will most undoubtedly never lift itself
      off the ground, all the weight of these people & the baggage we carry.
      All this cargo seems so important right now on this flight;
      it is all that is left, the only concrete thing to go back with me.
There were moments we shared that failed to matter,
      the visit to the Smithsonian (history seems so brief in the present &
      so temporary) The photo exhibit of couples in black & white

(nothing, except the lines on this page, ever exists in black & white)
But these, too, have passed, & all that matters now is the return flight,
the boarding back to my world that spins a bit slower,
where one does not fall in & quickly out of love.

This is the boarding & the boarding starts.

four letter words: hope

found hidden in the bed sheets
(as certain as fairies to children), though

he wasn't looking, per se, for the ocean's
last wave. he was looking, instead, for its ebb.

the quiet lull to & fro.
the gentle rocking in between

it all. that space where chaos
cannot enter despite its need to do so.

it was found in the dark skin, the brown
eye, the childhood friend, the slight new

york tongue, the greek mythology,
the immortal tattoo. the wet lip.

Diptych

i.   summer

the summer of this moment:
bodies locked forbidden.

stars as they rub themselves
over bodies like lotion on thirsty skin,

bowing overhead like parents
at the crib. & they will sing lullabies

until the morning sky splits open.
& we will embrace the summer sun

not as lovers but as thieves
who know only themselves in fits of hunger.

Diptych

ii.   autumn's awakening

& then
we have a red
maple growing
beside a white
oak, he said,
bowing his head
as lovers
often do
when going to bed,
autumn's scent
really meant
for growing boys
in corduroys
& birds & bees
& dirty knees.
i could say
i wildflowered,
though the image
is feminine,
it catches the power
when i devoured
the thoughts
he fed me
in a single hour—
the length
& strength
of the day
carried away
summer's being
& everything.

ebb

is it the mindlessness of childhood that opens up the universe?
            nothing happens anymore in a gas station.

newspapers open & close & feed the world
            all it needs to survive one more day.

a mosquito lands on my arm & i do not shoo it away.
            it is not lost; it is not found. it simply is.

the way the sun is. the way the tree in my front lawn is.
            the way time is as it taps me quietly on the shoulder.

have you grown too old to listen? the man asks.
            the wind was never one to stop talking.

i've grown too old to listen. i do not tell him this.
            instead i nod as if nodding were an answer,

knowing all the while that carousels were built only for children
            & young lovers & i am no longer either of these.

knowing all the while that dust will continue to fall
            & footsteps do not sound the same walking backwards.

i nod, as if living all alone on an island, pondering the same
            question over & over & over again:

is it the ebb of the tide as it returns to the sea, or is the sea
            consuming the wave?

song for the living
for dad

i. denial

the days are beautiful. flax
taking in wind taking in sun
taking in the rapture of a summer
sky. clouds never move
when watched closely. there is
a hole in the landscape
& we fill it with an inventory
of countless treasures: fresh
rose petals, black & white photographs
of uniformed men/bridal-gowned
women/jewels seaweed-hidden
along the atlantic coast.
the days are always beautiful,
& the nights live on forever.

ii. anger

days were beautiful. soot-covered
grass as though it were
an inseparable shadow. the umbra
of whatever is left
when love no longer breathes.
time is nothing
                but sorry it was ever born
because in the end there is no
difference between ash & dust:
the fist a terrible universe, a curse
in itself in air or in pocket,
a hinge-rusted vessel by which
we access our wrath
on those nights that live on forever.

iii. bargaining

if the days could be beautiful, if
the years could roll themselves out
like gold carpets, if God himself could
put his finger on a pulse & flow

life into hungry veins like tributaries
following their own current, if
red could turn to green come twilight, if
we could carry our medals on our
shoulders as the world cheers us on, if
we could cast our lance at death's
runaway steed & strike a blow
so hard it separates rider from horse, if
this were remotely possible, then
this night would last forever.

iv. depression

is a day that lost its will to be beautiful.
a disconnect from those things
that green from the very process
of greening. photosynthesis—
a lesson in history, the eye
no longer able to block the light.
the light no longer able
to stave off darkness. somewhere
in a cave as vast & wide
as a mountain beneath the ocean
a cry echoes
the same words over & over:
            this night will live on forever
            this night will live on forever.

v. acceptance

the days are beautiful & they
are not. they come to show themselves
for what they really are: a petri dish
where molecules of flesh & dust
collide in atmospheric rhythm. yet
we feel none of it—we become
cubes of ice, nebular particles
water-massed & hanging in the air
over the landscape in silent submission.
the world unfolds, becomes a series
of things that live & things
that don't: a frozen gaze that now
turns to the west. a once ageless
night that no longer lives forever.

Let us remember

lily pads floating in brooks we crossed
as children every Saturday in the park

when the evening sky grew dark & we
ran from our shadows in the headlights.

Two separate shades from two separate
trees you touched me like a summer breeze

when all the while you tightened a notch
in your belt, saving your breath to good-bye.

& were we not too young to fill our minds
with ferris wheels & naked children baked

in suntan lotion trying not to confuse emotion
with grief? Or were our words merely words,

as words can all too often be, echoing the sounds
of a wishing well full of penniless dreams?

Let us run beneath the blinking sunlight—
beneath the blinking streetlight careful not to step

on cracks in the pavement. Playing caveman
we swing our clubs with such passion & desire

summer light became winter fire, dancing our
way home in the falling rain, always failing

to be there before the streetlights came on. In
a later day I look outside, an old man leaning

on the same window sill I once sat on as a boy
whose feet dangled in the night counting footballs

& passing cars, wondering why, even in summer,
I have Christmas presents still wrapped, waiting

in the corner for people I may never again see.
Waiting, like an invisible child with his hand

in the air, the angel whose golden halo
has turned to tattered hair, waiting there.

Experiment

Eyes closed.
He tells time by the sound

of the crickets singing
their warning songs.

Pig, neck outstretched, slaughter-ready.
Pig not of plastic on a toy

farm from childhood, but
antiseptic white, like the flag

he waves to the virus
marching across his body

in an army of green. Pig of science,
& drugs pretty like gumdrops.

He lives not in the days of
scalpels: Sodium

Pentathol blowing into
veins like helium into a

balloon, witch doctors
& medicine men taking

lives, trekking miles across
the western world to throw

a worthwhile something into his
veins, the cure-all, the magic

whose name no one knows.
He is told his skin may percolate.

Coffee-rash. Nothing.
& he curls himself inside himself,

a paranoia, rocking back &
forth on his own hinges,

clinging to himself like a
hamster. Only bigger.

Quatrains for the Newly Unsexed

I.   The Kiss

It was all part of the experiment
of dating, of seeing if we, as boys,
could somehow lend our lips for merriment
amidst the autumn dirt & corduroys.

We came to learn that we preferred the lips
of boys against our own. The lesson made
itself known like the moon to the eclipse
& we shivered, but we were not afraid.

We kissed until our mouths flared & burned red
embers, jaws taut & tired, gasping for air.
Until the muscles in our faces bled;
our breathing the only sound we could hear.

Now they have the nerve to tell us kissing
is no longer safe. Imagine the tongue
a deadly weapon while reminiscing
about the days when you & I were young.

II.   Displaced

Everything is a time bomb—lips, tongue, hand,
saliva, eyes, blood, throat, finger, mouth, skin,
fist—& yet we are to remain human
& keep all our desires hidden within.

We've created a new closet, returned
to the milksoppy days of holding hands
on park benches, weakened by all we've learned
of the body & its hidden demands.

But the body demands adventure, lest
it become a barren & deserted
terrain, an unknown ghost town dispossessed
of pleasures still considered perverted.

Instead we tread the landscape of desire
deprived of wonder & fascination
like refugees seeking a Messiah
to offer us more than masturbation.

Ballad of the Little League Star: A Self-Portrait
(In Memory of Reginald Shepherd)

It never was the same, of course, except it never changed for him,
      when the others gathered together in one shower stall after the game, lined up
      like prisoners in a concentration camp, all in line, all single file, all waiting
      for the hand behind the barred window to stretch out & pass the next white towel.

That moment lasted forever. It is lasting still. He is there, thirty-five
      now, watching the boys hide themselves from each other.
      That is what they still are—boys—despite the hair around their
      nipples, despite the erections they cover with lather & towel,
      despite the fact that they look down at each other in anticipation
      & competition, knowing that they will not talk about this for weeks.

They are still boys despite the jock strap, the thickened muscle,
      the deep voice, the hairy knuckle, the Adam's apple. Still
      boys, with lunch bags packed by their mothers each day.

It never was the same, of course, except it never changed for him,
      when the others decided they did not want him on their team,
      never asking him about his undefeated record, his .666 batting
      average, his size 10½ cleats, his ability to hit a home run
      from both the left & right side of the plate.

They noticed instead his eyes as they roamed the locker room benches,
      his head as it bowed in silent secret, the extra time he took
      to fold & unfold his clothes. The dirt washing away on the shower tile.

four letter words: farm

Perhaps if, at nine, he continued to play
with the plastic farm set which he came

to know like a second alphabet. or perhaps
if, by not following his godfather as he

called to him in secret like in a game
of hide-&-seek, one hand on his mouth,

the other on his zipper, he would not be living
or dying the way he is. There was no clock

ticking among the chickens in the silo, no
disease on his farm in the country. He

should have known by the locked bathroom
door. The scent of the porcelain cold

like the tile around him. The clawed feet
of the bathtub as they gnawed at his knees.

The feeling that he should not enjoy the touch
of that white hair, fine yet coarse like fiberglass,

as it paid attention to his hips & much more.
The way the voice hesitated to say, *Very well,*

when his mother asked from the kitchen how
he was behaving. How the eyes looked red

like the wine in the glass for the rest of
the night, for the rest of his life. Or the way

he was returned like a prisoner to his cell
with underwear stained & backwards.

Temptation

The motionless ceiling fan in the dead of summer or
the cartilage that tears away at my septum or

the way summer carried himself into autumn
dressed in blue jeans & a red flannel shirt.

The last song that played in the jukebox at the bar
on the end of the street when the locals went home

after endless hours of shooting pool & gossip.
The smell of salt air on rustic New England roads.

The red of the maple leaf before the first frost or
the three ice cubes remaining in the empty glass

on the counter before the bartender discards it
without contemplating its history for just a moment.

The Jesus that followed me to class at the castle
on the edge of town. The accent in his voice or

the poetry that dripped from his pen in couplets or
the smell of Portuguese bread baking in the alleys.

The way his head now turns when I look him in the eye or
the sound of bodies releasing a seven year sigh or

his calloused fingers as they trace the outline of my lips or
the coffee grounds that connect evening to morning.

Desire

It lies awake
lonely in its folded
            skin.

Broken wing recalling
the day when it was
            God.

Unleashed to the world,
a giant. Too alive to be
            afraid.

This thing gnaws at us,
gnaws as if we were
            trees,

alive only to feed the ants
who gather at our
            feet

& carry our bark like
skin because they can. It
            gnaws

until our flesh is raw, until
we are no better than the
            snake.

faith

a portuguese man
who loves a man
is neither a man
nor portuguese
for he has been
too long away
that is what they say
yet they embrace pessoa
and shout he was their best
and erect a statue for him
on the busiest street
on the busiest hill
in lisbon, and when asked
why did sá-carneiro
succumb to strychnine
by his own hand
all they can offer is
he was an artist
haunted by his own soul
besides he lived in france
we are complex creatures
catholic miracles
pave our path
and we believe enough
to walk on our knees
and blame ourselves
when our beloved lady
of fátima passes us by
and we believe enough
in miracles like blood
raining from the sky
yet a portuguese man
who loves a man
is neither a man
nor portuguese

four letter words: blue

Why was I born on Monday, a small blue thing, a marble, a stone? Lapis lazuli in the garden of my youth. And why was it in June, under a silent blue-grey moon, when a brown boy took my hand and said, *The only thing you have going for you are your blue eyes*? And when I lay my head to rest, and the blue leaked out of my eyes and stained my bedroom pillow, why was I left white and barren? Did it have anything to do with the first crayon I used in kindergarten, the Siamese cat I had as a child, the turquoise ring shaped like a horse's head, the bluegrass music spit out by the radio when I delivered newspapers in the cold, or the ribbon I wore when I won the spelling bee? *You'll grow up to be a doctor,* my parents said as we picnicked and ate almonds under the willow tree, *because your eyes are blue.* So why is it? Exactly what caused it to be so that, instead of doctor, I grew to be patient and everything in my world is still blue? How can it be that the ink I use to sign my name when I fill my prescription, the Blue Cross/Blue Shield insurance card, the veins in my arms, and, because I washed them again with my jeans, my underwear, even the subway line in Boston that took me to the airport to say goodbye to my lover, the sky, just before the tornado, somewhere between green & indigo, when it twists itself in a shady knot & hovers over the earth, waiting, asphyxiated, taking an extra moment before the exhale, the body when it drowns just before dying & the fear in our eyes are all blue? Even today, Minnesota in February, under the dying streetlight, the snow's white looks faintly bruised.

Preparing for HAART

bottled words slurred from too much
pain & insomniac rituals

unsuccessful attempts to relieve
himself of all this time & energy

unable to wash away this virus crack
it open like a capsule & watch its

tiny globes spill & meander helplessly
harmlessly into other orbits

not yet occupied. his world right now
a quiet world a dying world a blue &

white capsule. sea & air wrapped in
a permeable shell locked inside like

the virus itself that shall explode
from within like pocked skin. this

is what it is like when the ink well
runs dry. when the noises from our bodies

lose their voices & what we have left
is all this time hidden in a cell of gelatin.

The Thing That Stirs
(lessons in dementia)

The small tap tapping of
the lead on paper.[1]

The buzzing of fruit flies
on plums.[2]

The TV guide with programs
circled in red;[3] strings on fingers,[4]

readjusted watches,[5]
& baseball schedules.[6]

The newspaper stories
repeating themselves each day.[7]

Newly released movies
she claims she's seen before.[8]

The thing that stirs
is a quiet thing,[9]

[1] It is not uncommon, when thinking or conjuring memory, to tap feverishly with a nervous tic. It helps, they say, to pass the time.

[2] After all, what other type of fly would hover over fruit?

[3] It is not entirely certain, but many believe that circling an item on paper stirs the memory to capture that item in isolation, as if it were a snapshot.

[4] Jewish mnemonics: Numbers 15:38-40. Bid them that they make them fringes in the borders of their garments … And it shall be unto you for a fringe, that you may look upon it, and remember all the commandments of the Lord.

[5] Even with batteries watches have a way of readjusting themselves so it is never the correct time. Still, as a wise man once said, Even a broken clock is right twice a day.

[6] If Young America is playing Green Isle, we know it must be a Sunday in summer. That is the only timeline we need.

[7] She takes the newspaper with her each morning, guards it in the pit of her arm like a running back guarding pigskin. Over time, the newspapers all share the same fate.

bouncing itself off the walls
of this house[10] slowly,

gently like a soap bubble.[11] It starts
upstairs, in the bedroom[12]

next to the den, where it crawls
along the carpet[13] & inches its way

to the drapes that hang
where the doors once stood.[14]

& carefully, with a surgeon's
precision it creeps downstairs.[15]

Memory comes in pieces, a leaf
at first, then a twig, never the entire tree.[16]

Nevermore.

[8]I've seen this movie a couple of years ago, back when I lived in Waconia, she says at the opening of
The Forgotten. We nod, understanding there is a logic we've yet to understand.

[9]Except when it is stirring in the wee hours of the night like a nocturnal vampire. Otherwise, it is
memory, silent and deadly

[10]The Wailing Wall. The Great Wall of China. No, the Berlin Wall—that's it. She's full of stories of
Germany and World War II. The Berlin Wall it is . . . now, where were we?

[11]Have we mentioned that she hides bars of soap in her closet, storing them for emergencies?
Wrapped like babes in swaddling tissue clothing.

[12]Her universe is now 13 feet long by 9 feet wide.

[13]The cleaning woman assigned by the county will clean this room, too, since it is considered com-
munal space.

[14]Drapes don't creak when you open them, and besides, you cannot lock yourself behind one.

[15]Flashlight in hand, like a camper unfamiliar with the camp.

[16]A family tree—species genetic.

One Sentence

I learned it all from first grade to fifth when I learned the components of a sentence, when I learned that the beauty of language is that we are all part of that language, that as we study what it means to be a noun, or a verb, or an adjective—all things I will reveal later—we also, simultaneously, as if the universes of emotion and alphabet were suddenly fused into one, we also *feel* what it means to be a noun, or a verb, or an adjective, and at that moment of fusion, when life becomes the word on paper, I finally come to terms with my life: a sentence, a line of words strung together sometimes with meaning, sometimes without meaning, always containing those things a sentence always seems to contain, like a noun, a common noun at that, like *faggot* (as in *God hates a faggot*, but not as in *God hates your faggot ways* because then I am no longer a noun, but an adjective, and that, you will find, comes much later in life), so instead my life, at this moment, is a noun—sometimes a common noun but then sometimes a proper noun (as in *Tommy*), or a compound noun (as in *twinship*), or a collective noun (as in *the genes that made us this way*), or a possessive noun (as in *I am and I will always be, my brother's keeper*); and only once when I am a noun, whether it be a common noun or a proper noun or a collective noun or a possessive noun—something inside me yearns to be, something inside yearns to give the nouns in my life meaning, and it is only when the desire to be burns inside like an ember struggling to stay lit do I suddenly unfold and become a verb—an inactive verb today (to be, as in *I am gay*), an active verb tomorrow, as in *replicate* (like carbon copies, or identical twins, or infectious viral particles); and as a verb I will be a variety of tenses, sometimes more than one simultaneously, sometimes just present (*I have AIDS*), sometimes present continuous (*I am trying to tell you I have AIDS*), sometimes just past (*I tried to tell you I have AIDS*), and sometimes future (*I will die with this disease*); regardless of which, I can be one or I can be all, but I will always be tense, and once I've seen myself as noun and verb I will slowly grow into adjective to describe myself and make myself more interesting to you, my audience, so that you will no longer see me as *your twin* but instead will come to know me as *your gay HIV-positive twin*, and to the parents who once knew me as *their son* I will be remembered as *their sick son*, sick from too much language and too much love, adjectives can do that to a person, and sometimes the adjective I become is multiple in meaning, and so I am split (as in *zygote*) and split (as in *personality*)—the adjectives I become can be confusing to a person; the adverb, on the other hand, disassociates itself from the subject and marries itself instead to its action; so, whereas I love, I can now love too *deeply*, and whereas I cry, I now cry *passionately*, and when it comes to loving, and when it comes to crying the sentence of my life takes on objects, and when those objects are direct I no longer love too deeply, instead I love *you* too deeply, and when those objects are indirect I no longer cry passionately, I cry passionately only *for you*, and so it is, as is the case with most twins, that the components of my life take on meaning and structure, and my life becomes the very sentence I use to describe it; yet like a sentence, as in the string of words full of subject and predicate, my life, too, is another sentence, a prison sentence, as in removed from the outside world, a sentence as in a final verdict, a judgment, a lack of freedom, or a loss of freedom once owned, a life once held in the palm of my hand and then taken away, forever, leaving me with only a series of words never without a verb to follow; otherwise, if I could, I'd be *individual* or *asexual* or *undetectable*: words all by themselves— words, ironically, only befitting a prisoner.

four letter words: eyes

The man's face was blue when he said it. *It's in our eyes like tiny specks of cotton. It's even in our tears.*

So is it any wonder that one day the world presents itself in high resolution & the next day everything seems clouded & grey?

The E on the top of the chart is really an F:

> Fires glow.

> Fires dance, stay still, dance again.

> Flowers in the garden die,
>   yet still we water them.

Yet we would rather say we have seen the light than face our inevitable death:

> The moon hiding in the background.

> The stars blinking with their own eyes.

> The feeling of faith: time turned on its side.

> > The feeling of love:
> > hair, nape, lip against
> > cheek. The glow of
> > skin against fingertip
> > shining like a coin in
> > a stream, one
> > perfectly complete
> > union—interlocking
> > like the original sin.

> The spirit as concrete as flesh.

four letter words: week

I learn to hold my grief inside my chest carefully, as if it were a glass lung, agreeing to tell no one about this. *The first week is the hardest,* I tell myself. *Survive it, and the rest will follow.*

But everything was over the moment he whispered with a voice as uncertain as it was broken, *I no longer want to be married. And I no longer want to be married to you.*

He said this as if marriage is what it was.

And wasn't it? Granted, we *were* two men, but there was also a church ceremony, with over a hundred witnesses. There were candles lit, and songs sung, and prayers spoken, and hands held. Vows were cited. Houses bought. Beds shared.

And there was a knot so tight even God couldn't untie it.

This is the way it happens, that first night, after the whisper:

day one

He says, *Let's spend tomorrow creating separate bedrooms.* And I agree because I know there is nothing else I could do. With the sky hanging low and heavy in my hand like a wet tea bag, I agree, hoping tomorrow will never come.

And I spend all day preparing for the last night we will sleep together. And I wonder, *Will we spoon one last time?* Wonder, *Will it be the sound of his breathing or the sound of my heartbeat that keeps me up all night?* Think, *Will our bodies repel each other like broken magnets, or will they embrace each other once more for old time's sake?*

And I cry. Four times to be exact, because crying is the only thing that seems natural. *Crying is for sissies,* I was told as a child, as if that moment of goodbye were predicted even back then.

And so I stall my arrival back home. Decide to work an extra hour. Go to the gym to run for 30 minutes hoping the endorphins will somehow save me. Stop to pick up dinner for the two of us, taking the long way home before eating it at the kitchen table as if there were no meaning at all in this pathetic ritual. And later in the evening, when the hour comes to go to bed, tomorrow arrives a day early. While I was working—trying desperately to hide the inevitable—he had already taken the liberty of preparing his own room. And I try not to notice as he enters it, closes the door behind him, and says nothing.

Not even, *good night.*

day two

I forget what to do with my mornings. *Divorce will do that to you,* a friend consoles me, but consolation is too far away and divorce reserved for other people. I fill the tank with gas, drive around until I run low. Fill it up again, drive around. Pull over on the side of the road to shake and cry and repeat to myself, *How did this happen? How did this happen? How did this happen?* I find myself in my own private seizure, and feel both afraid and pathetic.

It is winter in Minnesota, but I walk around the lake anyway. Go to the local animal shelter and notice a dog I want to adopt. *She's broken, like me,* I say to myself, but then deny myself the thought.

How can you think about adding to your life, I say to myself, *when you need to start subtracting?*

Another day. Another loss.

I am told this is what it is like.

day three

I am invisible. There is that feeling that I should matter, but I do not. Friends forget me. Family ignores me. The only constants are the answering machine greetings and the cold, falling snow outside.

Ten years together have come, sadly, to this.

Gone are the meals together, the movie theaters, the yearly vacations, the family visits. These were the things I could not stop thinking about. The loss eats away like a virus, and the obsession started here.

      No here.   Or here.

The problem, from the onset, you see, is that it is vast. So vast a page cannot contain it. And letters grow into words grow into sentences grow into paragraphs grow into chapters grow into complete or incomplete thoughts: the pen is so dangerous.

And none of this matters, because no one is listening but me.

day four

I know of no other place to go except the places we went together, but being there does not feel right without him. He has become my compass, my travel companion, my tour guide, my reason to sleep, my alarm clock, my reason to face the next day.

In a word, he was my life.

day five

Words repeat themselves like rain on April meadows. Words. Words repeat. Repeat themselves. Words repeat themselves like rain. Like rain. Like rain on April meadows.

It will never be this way again.

day six

Here, before the therapist, I share my thoughts as though I am all alone:

Mornings, by far, are the most difficult. Especially early, black-stilled-sky mornings. A force weighs me down into my bed. Another pushes, all the while reminding me that the world, in all its cruelty, does not stop to allow the catching up. The paper still arrives with the expectation that I will read the article *Should Gay Marriage Be Legal?* And I scoff at the twisted meaning in it all. *If there is no gay marriage, how could there possibly be a gay divorce?*

So instead I draw my attention to the bills—in both names—that arrive in the mail asking to be paid.

I don't always remember to exhale with each inhale.

Expecting as much would be heresy.

day seven

And here is what I want to say: Nothing has meaning anymore. Not the writing awards. Not the men whose heads I turn, nor the friends I want to inspire. I am too numb to find reason in any of it. Nothing has meaning anymore, and I never intended to live a life without meaning.

Divorce, they say, will do that to you.

Levitation
(for rené)

all you wanted was to rise,
for words to be enough to lift
your hands above your head, baring
thin-veined wrists, waiting for the world
to lick that skin clean. all you wanted
was to rise above it all feather-bellied.
the ascension, soft and prayer-simple.

there were words that soared
like pearl-white birds, clouds, both
time- and weight-immune. and your sky,
vast and too immense to contain them.

but when the voice sings,
gravity itself succumbs to its rope.
the feet, unaware, never touch the ground.

Making the Monster

I've had my holiday.
My day of being tied down.

Like Gulliver.
Like Jesus.

Bound by the world.
As if an experiment.

In sexual perversion.
At my side a book.

A gift from a priest.
Inside the words of Dollimore:

Perversion is an identity socially produced.
I've had my day.

Opened myself to society's probe.
A thing dissected.

To its atom state.
Microscopic.

I've lost my way.
Strangers lick their lips.

Point away from the center.
It is all part of the process,

I silently remind myself.
Pieces of me scattered.

The floor pocked.
I claim my day.

Not monster.
Not martyr.

Not virgin.
Not whole.

Reconstructed.
Pieces discarded.

A piece unused.
Reconstructed.

two

Lesson

What defines a life when you're a twin?
You tap your toe on the crib three times,

and by the third time he will always tap back.
This is what the tapping is like.

You wear a shirt of one color and that color
begins with the first letter of your name.

If your first name is *Tommy*
you will live a life of tans and teals; this is where it all starts.

And he, too, wears the same shirt, but of a different color,
perhaps blue, royal blue, navy blue, sky blue,

baby blue. His name begins with the letter *b*
because he was born first.

You hide alone in closets, and when guests visit
on Sunday you hide under the staircase covered

with wallpaper of flower riots and leaf-fallen trees.
In the bathroom until someone notices—someone doesn't always notice.

You sleep in the same bed as if sleeping in the same bed
were akin to sleeping in the unopened womb.

And listen late at night for noises that he makes
so you can listen to yourself when you're asleep.

Years later, when the cells stop working,
long after the roles have been defined

and the friendships have been made
and the lovers have been lost,

long after the world leaves you
finger-pointed and gasping for breath,

you take him in, all ten billion pieces of him,
and wrap yourself around him desperately like a strand of DNA.

You are living proof that no one is ever alone.
And so is he.

Rapunzel

It is as if the sky disrobed
himself before me of all

this futile snow. Like a lover
he allows me the simple

pleasure of making my footprint,
of caressing his silken body

with a cool wet touch.
This is what I have:

a mastiff that doesn't move,
a house that shouts from all corners

like an antichrist, & a clock
that reminds me every fifteen minutes

that my skin will soon turn
to leather. Some see the grave

with jellyfish & coral reef.
I see it filled with passion & sorrow,

a tower far & distant
untouchable as Rapunzel,

that sweet hermit with the golden
hair. My tomb is this house.

It stills my breath & seals me
from the world of touch.

Even when my hair was short
he'd say, *You're beautiful,*

& wink his eye & wave
like a white gloved prince.

I let down my hair
& even the snow melts away.

triptych

i.   *our adult souls*

like used gauze on dead

tree-

-lined streets littered runaway boys
& ice cream trucks each outrunning

the other

side of darkness a blinking streetlight,
reminded us that evening came even in

summer

when wiffle ball games ended in parking lots, & we
tired players carried our music on our shoulders like

heroes

whose echoes were once laughter, singing,
name calling, sticks & stones & such.

triptych

ii.   *betrayal*

like ten
perfect little indian boys
my fingers
                have betrayed me.

they've torn
the soul i had as a child
into tiny pieces
                & hid them

among fire trucks
& legos. my soul is now haunted,
ripened, lined
                with cobwebs & dead trees.

instead
of a blinking streetlight i see darkness.
instead of the laughter of children
                    i hear echoes.

triptych

iii.   *forgiven/wet*

i have somehow
erased my adolescence

                    like a forgiven sin,

blinked my way
through thirteen & twenty: from

                    building houses

out of cardboard boxes
& hiding deep within

                    the bowels

of the family closet
feeling something

                    like an ice skate

pierce my skull
& leave me bleeding

                    in silent lobotomy

dripping among
barbie doll cases

                    & has-been easter

dresses never
responding to voices

                    as they called my
name

& bounced
off every wall

                      like a rubber
band, to

standing alone
in the registration line

                  watching others

with faces stretched
like questions marks

                  following orders

like robots
freshly oiled

                  finely polished

feeling the weight
of the world

                  like a wet sin.

Cedar

We laugh from within
because inside we carry
the Cedars of Lebanon:
  (those warm greens wrapped
  in chains . . . prisoners
  awaiting their sentence).

& out back
our garden shrivels
like the evening sky
at the first hint of sunlight.
  (a desert
  a concrete lot
  & never, ever green).

But we climb trees.
Grab onto their thick muscular
trunks & swing from their
narrow branches like children
only bigger. & we laugh
blindfolded to the sky
as it drips quietly into night.

This is the closest we've been
to those mountains in Beirut
half-shaven in fright,
half-dressed in moon.

couplets for a shrinking world

it could have been the rhythm of the music
as it poured from the walls like honey

or the decision to not leave our little
universe until the evening moon gave

us its cue, or perhaps it was that something
electric that shot from your eyes

as you smiled, & watched me
watch you from afar. all i know

is i clenched my fist, to
capture the universe of that moment,

as if to seize it forever. i
clenched my fist until it bled.

Seven Trumpets for the Living & the Dead
(The Awful Naming of Things)

I saw the seven angels who stand before God, and to them were given seven trumpets.
Revelation 8:2

i   They call this judgment day,
the day twisting to meet its end

& we all fall down, like toy soldiers
& we all fall subject to the awful naming of things.

This one virus.
This one war.

This one not really one at all.
The trumpet-thundered sky,

bed sheets rip in the middle of the night,
entire bodies set ablaze

& then we die.
This we once called home.

ii   There was Jim.
Jim who dreamt of his father fishing,

lover of the sea like all good Portuguese fishermen.
& in his dream the second trumpet not like music

to his ears, more like the siren of a hurricane warning
spotting a nor'easter, lava in its eye.

The vision started as cloud
& his father with the imagination of a child.

One moment castle.
One moment crater

hurling itself into the sea
smashing into ship & fish & his father

with a force strong enough to leave nothing but a mountain
of bones & wooden beams hanging like stalactites from the sky.

This is the dream he dreamt each day.
This is the closest he ever came to telling his father the truth.

iii   As a young man living in an old man's body
the young old man bends with the weight of a tree in winter,

too weak to even crush the snow. *But for a dead man
earth & sand are clean water,* the poet poets.

& so he was drinking when the third trumpet split
the sky, spat out a star as if to regurgitate

the meal it could no longer hold.
The worm inside him the only living thing.

iv   As a child I poked a hole in a piece of paper
& held it to the ground & watched the sun recreate itself

before my eyes. The eclipse came
minutes later.

The boy & I cheering loudly as if for the home team.
We muffled the sound of the fourth trumpet,

sun-shattered
moon-shattered

& the stars
light snuffed out like a match.

The eyes of that boy next to me lit up like forest fire.
The sky is trying to tell us something, he said,

& I imagined the softness of his curly hair
the scent of it under my nose as he looked for the crescent moon.

The blond on his neck like velvet.
We were a perfect, incendiary match.

v   Perhaps it will be like this.
There will be the sound of a herald announcing something grand—
a summer sale in winter
a cure for the immedicable

the birth of yet another savior or twin
& the trumpet will sing a victory song

(only it won't be a victory)
& the sky will send forth a key

& it will open the earth like a crypt
& it will open the earth like a furnace

& it will open the earth like a giant bee hive
& our savior, there, planning the sting.

vi   Reading Amichai I ask, *Is all this sorrow?*
So much land taken up to bury our dead.

So much love wasted. Love, both
problem & solution. Cause & effect.

In this graveyard, the bodies below my feet call out
& I hear the trumpet & see the fire,

smoke & sulfur of their words leaking out
steam-like & plague-ridden.

Yes, this is sorrow,
this awful naming of things.

vii   Sunrise after the last day of battle.
We are supposed to rejoice in this.

We are supposed to welcome our new home,
relish the rewards of servanthood,

remember our history
not as an open wound

but as a healed scar.
We are supposed to remember

that underneath our broken flesh
some great joy is hiding.

A child walks among streets strewn with litter
carrying a lily for the dead.

They call this Memorial Day.

12

Always there are numbers playing with themselves
like little boys discovering their puberty.

. . . months, each frighteningly older than the one before,
until together they reach their final year, brittle-boned, and winter cold.

. . . disciples followed that bearded man
         like sycophants to the bequeathed,

              starved & enveloped-stuffed,
              crystal-ball transparent.

. . . t-cells just shy of a diagnosis.
         Exactly one dozen. Little eggs numbered & all.

In the grocery store he stands confused
like Sexton making up her mind.

But he always checks the eggs, inspecting each
for cracks in their fragile shells.

September Loss

In August there was no such thing as September.
In September there was no such thing.

If you've come to say goodbye, he says, don't
bother with stories or silly songs about what life

was like before this happened. It's not our first crisis.
Instead remind us of things we don't yet know,

like how to make the man who lost the man he
loves stop beating his head against the wall,

wishing that the winter flakes would somehow
stack themselves upon each other and drown him

when he wasn't looking. Tell him not to think
of the towers as two lovers holding hands in the summer sky.

In August New York was the oyster
in their hands. New York was the sky

that stretched overhead like a crown, like a snow
dome that held them from east to west.

Soldier: A Battle Hymn
For Paul Monette

There is no scar at which we can look
back & say heroic like a Persian Gulf
soldier, *Remember the War of 1991?* But
we remember. We've seen the lesions
line up at attention one by one shoulder
to shoulder scattered shooting in open
field calling out melodious as taps
sound off one two sound off three four . . .
We've heard the sound of our scabs
dressed in army-issue green as they rip
open like a troop of thieves & take
away our beautiful skin & spill on us
like tear gas their drops of spoiled
righteousness . . . We've lost our sight
for the memory of a stock & barrel lay
triggers in our mouths bullets in our
blood now unable to recognize eyes &
smiles seeing instead something shadow
shining like medals of honor. *All our
lovers have gone AWOL* the poet writes.
All our lives discharged . . . This is our war.
Void of yellow ribbons & dollar-a-month
veterans' life insurance policies. Old Glory
now a term we use for life before the war
back when we were brave & bronzed when
the ¼-inch cut of our hair told us we'd live
to serve our country no matter what

How to Love a Poz Man

Scientists will tell you several things: First, they'll say that we vary in the way we respond to outside stimuli. (They'll be thinking of how we respond to virus.) They'll say, *Some stave off the virus for a very long time; others succumb to it right away.* Say, *Better to begin HAART treatment now,* to the man in the corner who cannot fall asleep. Say, *Better to hold off on treatment so that you have options in the future,* to the man who still drives himself to work each day. Scientists will tell you several things about a poz man's response to outside stimuli.

(They'll be thinking, of course, of how he responds to virus.)

What they will not tell you, and what they will not be thinking, is that the man who shivers from the cold, thin river of ice that flows through his veins knows more than anyone else how to make love. They will not tell you that he has learned out of lacking what it means to fully receive. That each infected and dying cell that now makes up his tired, deteriorating body—from the soft, wet pillow of his hungry lip to the perfect mound of flesh just below his belly—each individual cell has learned not to turn itself away from the warmth of another man. That after an endless string of exile he has learned to respond to whatever outside stimuli offer the slightest asylum.

When you touch him—especially at the soft curve of the shoulder where hair often refuses to grow—his skin will flutter like a featherless bird in the palm of your unsuspecting hand. You may even notice the tiny bumps flowing from his shoulder to the side of his torso, spilling onto his hip and down the inside of his leg. *I cannot begin to describe how good that feels,* he may say when you trace the path with your fingers. All you will do is touch him.

This is how a poz man responds to outside stimuli.

And when the skin that quivers just beneath your fingertips begins to feel as though it is going to explode or retreat—you won't know which—you will stroke it like a tender wound because it will seem the natural thing to do. And as you stroke it like a tender wound because it will seem the natural thing to do, his eyes will roll back into their sockets. And you will want to say, *I am here.* Want to say, *Your skin has a soul all its own.* And if you, too, are poz, you will want to say, *It's hard to tell where I end and where you begin.* But you say nothing because words have no place in this most holy of sanctuaries, and instead, you allow your fingertips to find those remote places where words only intrude.

And as his eyes roll back into their sockets, they will trigger that thing within his brain that tells his head to lean all the way back as if you are bathing him with your presence. And as his eyes roll back into their sockets, his mouth will open ever so slightly, and a breath too faint to hear will escape into the silent ether and beckon you to kiss him.

And you will.

And the kiss will begin with lip against lip, and your heart will race just short of seizure. Lip against lip and you will want to burst out of your skin. Lip against lip and the walls around you will develop their rhythm. Their own private heartbeat. Lip opening lip and tongue against impatient, unquenchable tongue.

And scientists will not tell you what happens next, so there is no way for you to know what to do when his body invites you to enter him the way a city too long silent suddenly invites sound. You think, *All this wonder in the palm of my hand.* Think, *He is as vast as an open field.* Think, *To be inside him is to meld with all his beauty and all his history and all his joy and all his pain.*

The intensity grows, and you think only of melding.

So you cover his mouth with your hand as you enter him because the unspoken rule has already established itself: words only intrude. And as you enter him, he will touch the soft curve of your shoulder where hair often refuses to grow, and your skin will flutter like a featherless bird in the palm of his hand. And tiny bumps will flow from your shoulder to the side of your torso, spilling onto your hip and down the inside of your leg. And you will want to say, *I am here.* Want to say, *Our skin has a soul all its own.* Want to say, *It's hard to tell where I end and where you begin.* And your eyes will roll back into their sockets, and your head will lean back as if he is bathing you with his presence, and your mouth will open ever so slightly, and a breath too faint to hear will escape into the silent ether.

succumbing to sleep

each night just before it comes he makes
sure he casts himself into that deep sleep
succumb to that sleep before he has a chance
to see it open its huge mouth & devour
him the way a tunnel devours a train but
there are times   & times all too often
times   when he faces the twelfth hour &
sometimes bold but not always   sometimes
unaware neglectful of the hour until
it sounds its threatening roar   cries like
church bells peal as they do on Sundays
tonight it is bewitching him   he is bewitched
just watch the hour toll each gong striking
down another T-cell   strip him of his only
ammunition only a temporary weapon in
this ephemeral fight   still the gong   still the
echo   like death calling out his name   & at
that evening-morning hour that slices the day
like an executioner seeking revenge it comes
with its ugly head rapping on his door   death
asks him to sign its contract   the beating of a
pulse trembles him he could not cross a t or
dot an i & still it smiles its slow painful grin
never to run out of ink there to wait until all his skin
is pocked until all his skin is pocked & peeling off

rigor mortis at twenty-six

happens only late in the evening
when all the stars blink in unison

& the sounds of the city echo
                                long past midnight

me: a corpse erection-stiff
or better yet a gangplank casting myself

into an angry ocean like an undercooked
                                piece of meat

i am fed to the sharks
they swim around me as if i were

it
in a game of tag.

Conversation with Jim on a Hill

not a hill more like a mound a plot of dead
land a patch of dirt & newly planted grass
laid out in this cemetery which spreads itself
like a quilt here on this patch just one week
before Memorial Day no not a week nine days
to be exact May 19 2001 here I sit on this patch
of dirt & newly planted grass something sacred
now because of you something which calls me back
from Minnesota back two thousand miles to the
Notre Dame Cemetery 1540 Stafford Road
Fall River Massachusetts Lot 73 Section 2
to a tombstone marked Viveiros your mother's
maiden name—who was it that once told me
that we Portuguese are really immortal that
death is just a phase we go through—how I wish
I could believe that now how I wish I could
believe that here on this same plot of dirt
& grass I visited nine years ago

There are flowers here for you flowers by your
plot many flowers tell me someone else has
visited you recently it was someone else not I
who left these flowers you see today instead I
hold a pamphlet of the Rules & Regulations
of the cemetery rules & regulations that say
all flowers placed at grave sites become the
property of the cemetery & will be used to
beautify the grounds & I think to myself
were you not enough to make this somber
place more beautiful were you not enough
that they need to take your flowers too

who was it who visited you last who else could
never forget the meal you fed me at that restaurant
on Thayer Street when my thumb was sliced
& sutured & bandaged so that I could not
even lift my fork or the way your shoulders
moved up & down like a man on a string
whenever you laughed or the beauty mark on your right
cheek which charmed the world like a newborn
babe or your eyes two chestnuts always looking up or
up to something was I not enough for you Jim

who else but I visited your classroom pretending
to take notes on the science of instruction instead
writing love poems which would never be read aloud
& who but I Jim shivered when you winked as your
students called you Mr. Correia who else Jim who else
visited you when you shriveled away & who asked
why do you watch the home shopping club so
much & you replied *it's the only company I*
have these days & now even now who else
but I stretch themselves upon this patch of land
your little plot of earth & offer themselves to you
just six feet above nine years later at this
cemetery plot two thousand miles away &
whisper prostrate arms stretched in crucifixion
Jim, dear Jim, you left this world too soon!

At this moment I want the world to stop turn
my gaze to the wind which blows east toward
the ocean cresting somewhere off these shores
I want to stop time for just a few moments I
want to but never could stop time instead the
ocean is cresting still the same way it did on
July 28 1992 at 17 Brigham Street in Rumford
Rhode Island the ocean is cresting still as if the
shores have suddenly forgotten what to do
Jim, I cannot stop this crest.

four letter words: cure

What would it be like if one of the doctors dressed in green scrubs from head to toe & a white overcoat confirming his authority came running into my hospital room, arms flailing as wildly as his stethoscope & announced, *My God, it worked! It really worked! There is no trace of HIV in your system at all* . . . ? What if this treatment proved successful, & instead of reminding myself that yes, the official diagnosis is—& will always be—AIDS, I would convince myself that my body is once again brand new? Would it be like the time when I was diagnosed with severe liver damage, & I sat in the bathtub & listened to a cassette tape of water trickling down a brook & imagined myself pouring a magical elixir over my sick grey organ, cradling it in my arms the way a mother cradles a baby, all the while washing it until it once again became a healthy pink color, & doctors proclaimed, *It's a miracle, that power of visualization!?*

I suspect it would be like a beautiful room that has just been emptied of all its fine furnishings—a luxurious carpet lifted over here; a sculpture of the living dissolving over there. There would be a mourning of sorts, having lived my life betrothed to my beloved only to find my beloved was now undetectable. There would be a mourning indeed.

I suspect I would have to learn to live again, a form of rehabilitation for the dispossessed.

notes written to a viral neighbor

day grows long so you wish it would die
  wish it would peel like a leaf from a tree

fall on the ground age in the sun form another
  ripple in the pond you wish it would die

& then feel it in the palm of your hand
  shedding its colors its laughter its

sorrow its winter you cannot pick it up
  & feel it & nurse it back to life like

an infant in a mother's arms & then still
  wish it would die

looking out my window i see you
  falling you almost bare yet full

of unpocked skin you get dressed & leave
  behind the life of someone else's misery

the idea that you are immune from the crisp
  air & the winter & although I cannot

hear you I see laughter spill from you like
  medicine in trembling hands now only your

shadow your body no longer exists behind the
  curtain just a shadow with your shape

a shadow—& nothing more—
  hours later you return to your lair like a beast

in search of shelter while the piano in my room
  begins its own requiem it caresses a full moon

tonight round & full like a golden calf or maybe
  it is for me i am not asleep at midnight scratching

off words instead of counting sheep *sleep is a lot
  like death* i write we trap ourselves in these cages

register ourselves to the train of thought that there
   is only one life   one death   one shadow we can cast

& still it lasts longer than we   & oh you now
   turn off our light   *was there too much there for*

you or not enough?   though it doesn't matter it is too
   small to see with the human eye

Dirge for an Entertaining Host

I
i welcome you,
nameless, bouncing from cell to cell
a prisoner who never learns how to die
only how to kill

II
hiding behind liquid & bone,
just enough to make yourself known

III
& whoever used the term *undetectable*
studied a different kind of math than you did
you, whose numbers multiply daily, you
you you you you you
my exponential you

IV
i try to imagine what you are like
what personality you have hidden behind
those vacant eyes
what it is like to love someone so small
yet so large at the same time
& i watch you as you swing
back & forth in my head
like a palindrome,
sometimes melodic like Sexton's
rats live on no evil star
other times haunting like a repeating burrow in my veins
and DNA and DNA and DNA

V
science tells the reader there are no words before it
faith tells science that there are
we read, regardless, with words in mind
because, even invisible, you breathe

VI
you & i
we, two, became one
& the poet asked,
When did that happen?

VII
you have lived with me for half
my life, more than family, more
than friends, more than lovers
will you ever tire of my ways?

VIII
That I should embrace you is, perhaps, the solution. That I should bring you
home to mother for Thanksgiving & Christmas & proudly wrap my arms
around you & say, *This is the one with whom I plan to spend the rest of my life, this
is the one with whom I will go to the depths of hell, this is he, my new family, who
needs me in order to survive.*

post mortem: an ode

tonight
over pineapples & tea leaves

we spoke smiles & poetry
& for one moment we wanted

that old kitchen table to crack open
& give birth to a new lazarus

who would speak to us in creole
& show us lights we couldn't see.

& we awaited
the slightest of sound.

crackle
warm fire.

hush
baby's breath.

but that old piece didn't budge.
even when we kicked its wooden

legs & prayed for momentum
it just stayed sat still,

statue-like,
& left us

with nothing
to wipe our eyes agnostic.

Ode to Pneumocystis Carinii Pneumonia
at the First Dosage of Aerosolized Pentamidine

These are not Gunn's night
      sweats I've read about:

cold, empty wet sheets—
      leftover tricks, nights of terror.

But still they just might
      make me live without

ever tasting sweet,
      regretting every error

like a pencil with no eraser—
      the silent race. The silent racer.

The nurse from Chartwell
      sighs, sterile-voiced,

You're protected now
      from pneumonia's evil wrath.

The tube begins its swell
      & as if by choice,

its plastic somehow
      chokes the way a psychopath

might, fear growing faster like a cyst—
      leaking itself into the unsuspecting mist.

grief *

it happens at first in the morning, before the sun has done its dirty job,
        when you least expect it is when it happens. your eyes,
        though alert, may even be closed.

& this is the way it happens: it leaks from you like sap from old trees,
        the drip slow at first—so slow you don't even notice the salt as it
        seeps from your eyes. there is no stain or residue

it just happens to be more invisible than that.

& once it empties itself,
        it crawls on the ground, surrounds your feet
        & every step you take has you bumping into things.
        a broken sidewalk over here. an extra step over there.
thoughts, iceberg-solid both above & below
        the ocean's surface.

i could have avoided these things. face stricken, i could have turned
        the other way when love opened its callous hand
        could have wrapped myself in the brittle leaves of autumn
        when no one was looking.

i had that chance to be invisible. but chose, sadly, to be seen.

* upon being inspired by a poem by Rachel Moritz

my barefoot soul

walks these corridors, steps on glass
the church says exists only in my mind—

broken like the family in the photo,
my thorn-pricked soul bleeds.

i'm told the blood i lose is not as real as that of jesus
so i could never understand a disease with no cure.

yet my auto-immuned soul still self-infects.
it is my albatross that hangs

heavy as a stone scapular.
it is my tree.

my emaciated body.
my unhealed scar.

my open tourniquet.
my broken soldier.

four letter words: fear

i'm not afraid of feelings hanging on me like suits
cadaver-black & napkin-starched. i'm afraid of words.

they stalk me—make me a blueprint, reveal all
my closets. locked doors. secret hideaways.

words have the power to become real.
Example: i must say i am ready. ready to waken one

minute past midnight limp & wet—cold fish in a sea
of bed sheet watching, waiting for the herons to fly low.

ready for the bumblebees to move marching-band
slow in my veins. the same march over

& over
& over again in their brass cacophony.

ready for my sky to crack open with a thousand & one violins.
for solitaire to go into overtime. for time to shine upon me

like a sundial, my shadow slowly getting smaller
in the west-setting sun.

for my hungry words to swallow me like an epitaph,
turn themselves into number.

i am ready to start counting backwards.

Acknowledgements

Many thanks—

to the editors of the following books and literary journals in which excerpts of this collection have previously appeared: *Gulf Coast* and *Other Words: A Writer's Reader* (One Sentence); *Water~Stone Review* (How to Love a Poz Man); *Hot Metal Press* (Washington Suite); *Swell* (One Week); *Gents, Badboys and Barbarians: New Gay Male Poetry* (Rapunzel); *Collective Brightness* (faith); *Windy City Times* (Ballad of the Little League Star); *Poetry Gallery of the Erotica Readers & Writers Association* (Pushing, from Washington Suite); and *Backspace* (Preparing for HAART);

to the editors of the following literary journals, where my writing has also appeared: *Sport Literate*; *Willow Springs*; *Evergreen Chronicles*; *Christopher Street*; *Chiron Review*; *The Talking Stick*; *Midway Journal*; *Big Toe Review*; *Marco Polo Quarterly*; *Two Hawks Quarterly*; *Writers Against War*; *Art & Understanding*; and *Perspectives*;

to Juliet Patterson, poet extraordinaire, for her many reviews and comments;

to Hamline University's outstanding MFA program, with its tireless faculty and staff;

to the Minnesota State Arts Board for believing in this project;

to my brother, without whom none of this would be possible; and

to John, my love, for his faith and deepest support.

John Medeiros is a fiscal year 2010 recipient of an Artist Initiative Grant from the Minnesota State Arts Board. This activity is funded, in part, by the Minnesota arts and cultural heritage fund as appropriated by the Minnesota State Legislature with money from the vote of the people of Minnesota on November 4, 2008.

about the author

Photo courtesy of MQARTWORK.COM.

John Medeiros is a poet and memoirist whose work has appeared in numerous literary journals. He is the recipient of two Minnesota State Arts Board grants; a Jerome Foundation Grant for Emerging Writers; Gulf Coast's First Place Nonfiction Award; and the AWP Intro Journals Project Award. His work has been nominated for a Pushcart Prize, and as a Notable Essay in Best American Essays of 2006. He is the curator of Queer Voices: A GLBT Reading Series, a reading series for queer writers sponsored by Intermedia Arts. More information about him can be found at his website, www.jmedeiros.net.

www.jmedeiros.net

Queer Voices: A GBLT
Reading Series

Facebook